Homes
Around
the World

Acknowledgments

Executive Editor: Diane Sharpe
Supervising Editor: Stephanie Muller
Design Manager: Sharon Golden
Page Design: Simon Balley
Photography: Bryan and Cherry Alexander: page 26;
Ancient Art and Architecture Collection: page 16; Image Bank: page 18;
Spectrum: page 22; Tony Stone: cover (left), pages 6, 10, 12, 14, 20, 24;
Zefa: cover (right) page 8.

Library of Congress Cataloging-in-Publication Data

Jackson, Mike, 1946-
    Homes around the world/Mike Jackson; illustrated by Jenny Mumford.
      p.   cm. — (Read all about it)
    Includes index.
    ISBN 0-8114-5727-3 Hardcover
    ISBN 0-8114-3741-8 Softcover
    1. Dwellings — Juvenile literature.   [1. Dwellings.]   I. Mumford, Jenny, ill.   II. Title.   III. Series: Read all about it (Austin, Tex.)
GT172.J33   1995
392.36—dc20
                                          94-29422
                                               CIP
                                               AC

1 2 3 4 5 6 7 8 9 0 PO 00 99 98 97 96 95 94

Homes Around the World

Mike Jackson

Illustrated by
Jenny Mumford

STECK-VAUGHN
COMPANY
ELEMENTARY • SECONDARY • ADULT • LIBRARY

People around the world live
in many different kinds of houses.

Let's go and see some of them in
the magic helicopter.

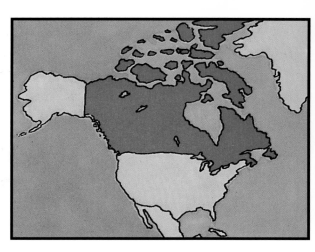

Now we have
landed in Canada
near the North Pole.

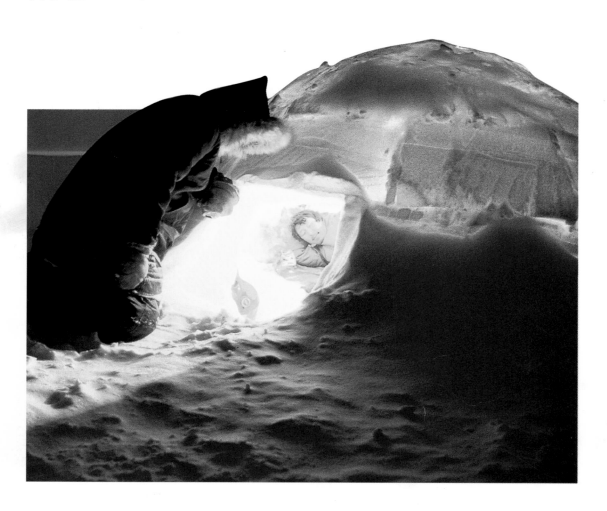

This is where the Inuit people live.

Many Inuits build igloos to sleep
in when they go hunting.

It must be
cold in there.

Igloos look cold, but they're really
warm and snug inside.

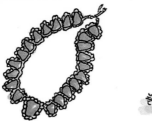

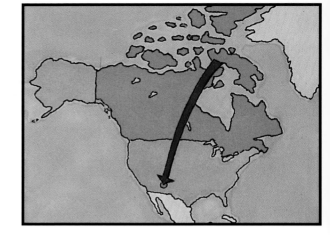

Now we are in
the southwestern
United States. These homes belong
to the Pueblos.

Many Pueblos live in adobe houses
like these.

Adobe is a name for clay bricks
that have been dried in the sun.

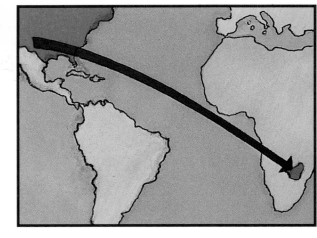

Now we're in Zimbabwe, a country in Africa.

Look! These houses are made from mud and leaves.

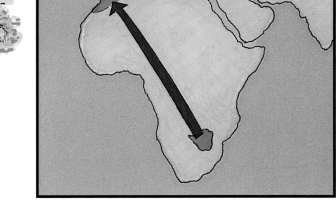

This is Morocco, another country in Africa. The houses here have flat roofs because there is very little rain.

The walls are thick, and the windows are small.

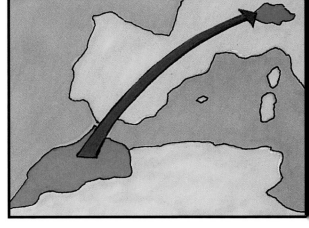

Now we are in the mountains of Switzerland. Many people live in chalets with gently sloping roofs.

The snow stays on the roof and keeps the house warm.

14

 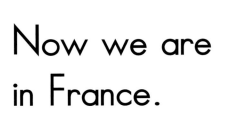

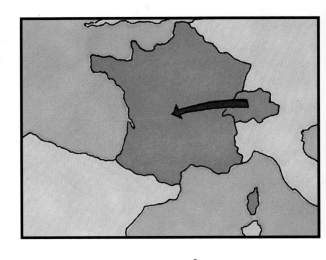

Now we are
in France.
Thousands of years ago, people
lived in these caves.

They painted pictures on the walls.

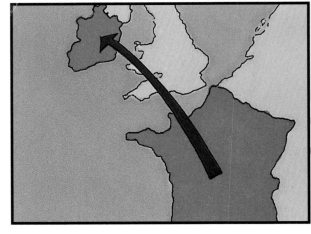

Now we are
in Ireland.
That wagon used to be the home
of a gypsy family.

19

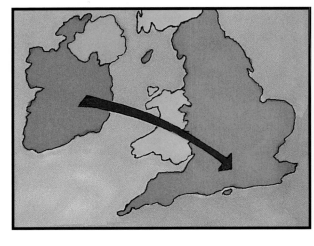

This pretty
cottage is
in England. It was built
400 years ago.

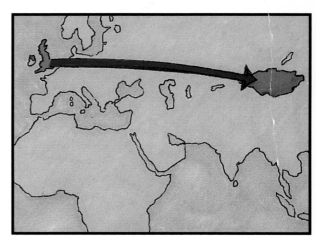

We are in
Mongolia now.
Those round tents are called yurts.

The people here are called nomads.
They move from place to place.

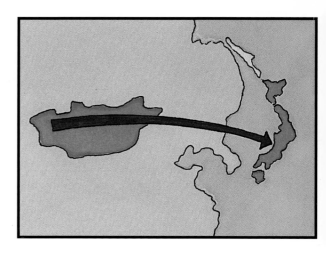

Now we are
in Japan.

In this house, the rooms are
divided by sliding doors made
out of paper.

24

This is Hong
Kong harbor.
Many of the people in Hong Kong
live on boats.

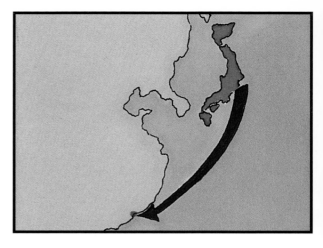

Here are some of the houses
the children saw on their trip.
Do you remember where each
can be found?

30

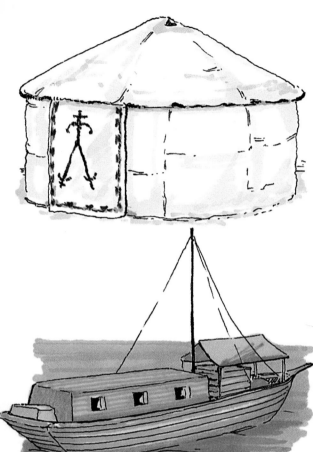

Index